TIME FOR KIDS®

CONFIDENT 3 READER — Science Scoops

Butterflies!

By the Editors of TIME FOR KIDS
WITH DAVID BJERKLIE

HarperCollins*Publishers*

About the Author: David Bjerklie is a science reporter for TIME magazine. He has written articles for TIME and TIME FOR KIDS® on health, nature, and geography. The author collected fossils, bugs, and fish as a kid and studied biology and anthropology in college.

To my very favorite two butterflies in the world, Erika and Sarah.

Special thanks to science teachers everywhere.   —D.B.

Butterflies!
Copyright © 2006 by Time Inc.
Used under exclusive license by HarperCollins Publishers Inc.
Manufactured in China.

Library of Congress Cataloging-in-Publication Data is available.

ISBN-10: 0-06-078213-7 (pbk.) — ISBN-10: 0-06-078217-X (trade)
ISBN-13: 978-0-06-078213-9 (pbk.) — ISBN-13: 978-0-06-078217-7 (trade)

1 2 3 4 5 6 7 8 9 10
First Edition

Copyright © by Time Inc.
TIME FOR KIDS and the Red Border Design are Trademarks of Time Inc. used under license.

Photography and Illustration Credits:
Cover: Alamy; cover front flap: Chris Martin Bahr—SPL; title page: Gail M. Shumway—Bruce Coleman; contents page: Michael & Patricia Fogden—Minden; pp. 4–5: Dr. John Brackenbury—SPL; pp. 6–7: Brand X Pictures/Alamy; pg. 7 (inset): E. R. Degginger—Animals Animals; pp. 8–9: Anne Reas; pg. 9 (inset): Anne Reas; pp. 10–11: Michael & Patricia Fogden—Minden; pp. 12–13: Klaus Nigge—Foto Natura/Minden; pg. 13 (inset): Patti Murray—Animals Animals; pg. 14: Scott Camazine; pg. 15: Scott Camazine; pp. 16–17: Frans Lanting—Minden; pg. 17 (inset): Scott Camazine; pg. 17 (How Big?): Anne Reas; pp. 18–19: Robert M. Vera—Alamy; pp. 20–21: Fritz Polking—Peter Arnold; pg. 21 (How Far?): John Berg; pp. 22–23: Rod Planck—NHPA; pg. 23 (inset): Breck P. Kent—Animals Animals; pp. 24–25: James L. Amos—Corbis; pg. 25 (butterfly inset): AP; pg. 25 (Chip Taylor inset): courtesy Chip Taylor/Monarch Watch; pp. 26–27: Brian Farrell/Museum of Comparative Zoology & Harvard University; pp. 28–29: Alan Blank—Bruce Coleman/Alamy; pg. 29 (inset): Monserrate J. Schwartz—Alamy; pg. 30–31: A. H. Rider—Photo Researchers; pg. 31 (inset): Gail M. Shumway—Bruce Coleman; pg. 32 (chrysalis): Frans Lanting—Minden; pg. 32 (endangered): A. H. Rider—Photo Researchers; pg. 32 (metamorphosis): Frans Lanting—Minden; pg. 32 (migration): Fritz Polking—Peter Arnold; pg. 32 (scales): E. R. Degginger—Animals Animals; pg. 32 (spinnerets): Scott Camazine; pg. 32 (Costa Rica): Corbis; pg. 32 (Ethiopia): Nathan Brockman—Reiman Gardens; pg. 32 (France): Naturfoto Honal/Corbis; pg. 32 (Indonesia): Michael & Patricia Fogden—Minden; pg. 32 (Russia): Pat O'Hara—Corbis

Acknowledgments:
For TIME FOR KIDS: Editorial Director: Keith Garton; Editor: Nelida Gonzalez Cutler; Art Director: Rachel Smith; Photography Editor: Jill Tatara

 Check us out at www.timeforkids.com

CONTENTS

Chapter 1: Flying Flowers 4

Chapter 2: Amazing Changes. 10

Chapter 3: Migrating Monarchs 18

Chapter 4: Long Live Butterflies! 26

Did You Know? 31

Words to Know. 32

This tree nymph butterfly is from Indonesia.

CHAPTER ONE

Flying Flowers

Swallowtail butterflies soar over a field of flowers.

Flutter! Flutter!

Something colorful glistens in the meadow. Is it a flower? No, it's a butterfly! Its beautiful wings flutter in the air. This creature is one of the insect world's biggest showoffs!

The blue morpho lives in the rainforests of Central and South America.

The wings of the blue morpho butterfly are not really blue. But when tiny ridges on the scales reflect light, the wings appear blue.

Butterflies and moths belong to the same group of insects.

Short hairs called scales cover their wings like powder. Some scales can even make the wings appear to shimmer. Butterflies are usually more brightly colored than moths.

Take a close look at a butterfly.

Butterflies are active during the day. They hold their wings straight up while resting. There are nearly 20,000 different types of butterflies.

FOREWINGS:
Butterflies have two front wings.

HIND WINGS:
Butterflies have two back wings.

BODY: Butterflies' bodies are divided into three parts: the head, thorax, and abdomen.

ABDOMEN

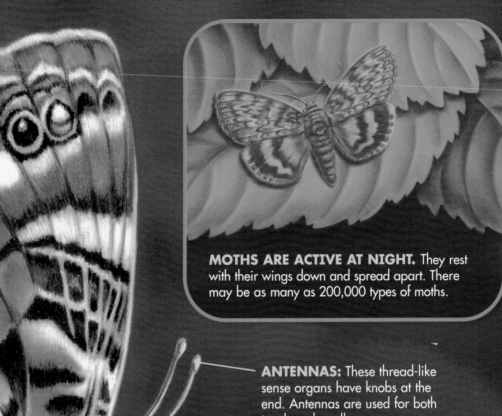

MOTHS ARE ACTIVE AT NIGHT. They rest with their wings down and spread apart. There may be as many as 200,000 types of moths.

ANTENNAS: These thread-like sense organs have knobs at the end. Antennas are used for both touch and smell.

HEAD

EYE: Two compound eyes let butterflies see in almost every direction.

PROBOSCIS: Butterflies use their long coiled tongues to sip water or nectar from flowers.

FEET: Special organs on butterflies' feet help the insects taste what they land on!

THORAX

CHAPTER TWO

Amazing

The pierid butterfly's eggs look like tiny jewels.

Changes

The life of a butterfly begins in an egg. Butterflies lay eggs one at a time or in clusters. They lay their eggs only on plants that caterpillars like to eat. That's because when an egg hatches, a caterpillar comes out!

An oriole gobbles
a caterpillar.

WATCH OUT!

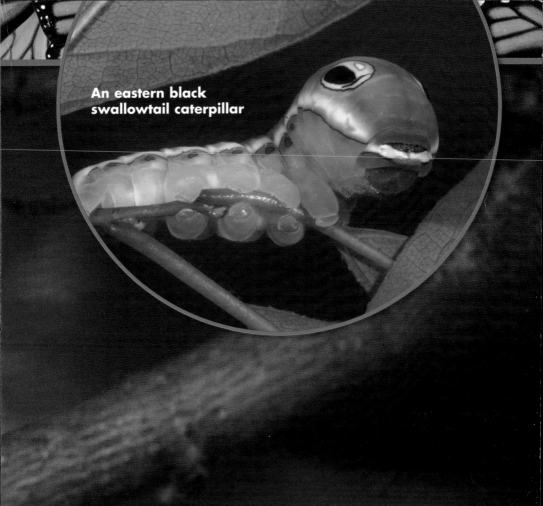

An eastern black swallowtail caterpillar

A caterpillar is tiny when it hatches.
Then it begins to eat and eat. It can eat many times its own body weight every day.
Caterpillars shed their skins several times.
This is called molting.

But caterpillars must be careful. It is a dangerous world for them! Most end up as a meal for birds, frogs, and other insects.

A monarch caterpillar attaches itself to a leaf.

HANGING OUT!

The chrysalis may hang on a twig for weeks or even months.

One day the caterpillar looks for a safe spot to make a home.

Then it sheds its skin one last time. With the help of special mouthparts, called spinnerets, it attaches itself to a plant, twig, or leaf. The caterpillar makes a case called a chrysalis.

The chrysalis changes color.

Inside the chrysalis an amazing change takes place.

It is called metamorphosis. First the chrysalis turns almost clear. Then it splits open. The butterfly struggles to get out. Soon it will fly!

At last the butterfly emerges.

How Big?

The Queen Alexandra birdwing, which lives in New Guinea, is the biggest butterfly. It has a wingspan of twelve inches.

The pygmy blue, which lives in the U.S., is the smallest butterfly. It has a wingspan of less than half an inch.

CHAPTER THREE

Migrating

Every year as many as half a billion monarchs make a long, dangerous journey south. Their migration begins at the end of summer. They need to find a new home for the winter.

Monarchs

Monarchs in California will head south.

Monarchs rest on a fir tree in Mexico.

Many monarchs head to a mountain hideaway in Mexico.

They will spend the winter in a forest of fir trees. It is a perfect place to rest because the air is cool and moist.

For more than four months, hundreds of millions of monarchs flock in the trees. The monarchs rest and wait for winter to end.

How Far?

Canada

United States

Mexico

Monarchs are long-distance travelers. It can take one monarch up to sixty days to reach its winter home. Some travel as far as 3,000 miles!

North

West ◄─┼─► East

South

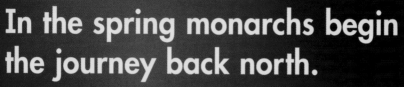

In the spring monarchs begin the journey back north.

Some are now more than six months old. This generation of monarchs lives longer than others. Most monarchs only live for about a month!

Along the route monarchs lay eggs and die. Caterpillars hatch from these eggs. The butterflies that develop continue the trip.

A monarch caterpillar crawls on milkweed, its favorite food.

Monarch eggs

It is summertime!

Northern areas are once again filled with monarchs. These are the great-great-grandchildren of the butterflies that made the long journey to Mexico.

Soon it will be time for monarchs to head south. How do they know their way? Scientists are working to find the answer.

These monarchs are in Louisiana.

Hail to the Monarchs!

Chip Taylor thinks monarchs rule. He is a scientist who studies insects. "The monarch migration is one of the world's wonders," says Taylor. "This butterfly weighs less than a paper clip, but it can fly for two months!"

Taylor is the director of Monarch Watch. Each year thousands of volunteers tag almost 100,000 monarchs. Numbered stickers are carefully placed on butterflies' wings. Volunteers must be gentle!

If you find a tagged butterfly, report it to Monarch Watch. The information will help scientists learn more about monarchs and their long journey.

Long Live

This ancient butterfly is preserved in stone.

Butterflies!

A butterfly may look delicate, but it is one sturdy insect. Butterflies and moths fluttered in the sky when dinosaurs roamed the earth. These gentle bugs have graced our planet for more than 150 million years!

An owl butterfly
has eyespots.

Butterflies don't bite or growl.

So how do they stay safe? Some butterflies
are poisonous. Others use camouflage to
blend into their background. Butterflies
with big eyespots on their wings scare
enemies away.

Plant a Butterfly Garden!

You can help butterflies by planting a garden that attracts them. Find out what butterflies live in your region. Then grow their favorite foods. Monarchs like milkweed plants. Swallowtails love pipevine. Many butterflies enjoy marigolds, bee balm, coneflowers, lilacs, and peonies.

Butterflies are attracted to bright colors. Purple, yellow, white, blue, and red are their favorites. Butterflies also enjoy sipping fruit juice. Watermelon, mashed ripe bananas, or strawberries make good snacks.

A yellow swallowtail lands on a marigold.

One hundred years ago, there were more butterflies than today.

Many species are endangered or extinct. We need to work to keep butterflies in our world!

Did You Know?

- Butterflies live everywhere except Antarctica.
- Butterflies cannot fly unless the temperature is above 60° F.
- Most butterflies fly at a speed of about 5 miles per hour. But some can fly as fast as 30 miles per hour!
- Some male butterflies are often so busy finding mates that they do not have time to eat.
- Many adult butterflies sip nectar from flowers. They help spread pollen from flower to flower. This helps flowers make seeds.

The karner blue butterfly is endangered.

WORDS to Know

Chrysalis: the protective case in which metamorphosis takes place

Migration: a seasonal journey

Endangered: animals or plants in danger of dying out, or becoming extinct

Scales: the tiny hairs that cover a butterfly's wings

Metamorphosis: the change by which a caterpillar becomes a butterfly

Spinnerets: special mouthparts that help a caterpillar make a chrysalis

FUN FACTS — HOW DO YOU SAY BUTTERFLY?

1 In **Costa Rica**, a butterfly is called a mariposa.

2 In **Ethiopia**, a butterfly is called a birrabirro.

3 In **France**, a butterfly is called a papillon.

4 In **Indonesia**, a butterfly is called a kupu-kupu.

5 In **Russia**, a butterfly is called a babochka.